William M. F. Petrie

Racial Photographs from the Egyptian Monuments

William M. F. Petrie

Racial Photographs from the Egyptian Monuments

ISBN/EAN: 9783337240332

Printed in Europe, USA, Canada, Australia, Japan

Cover: Foto ©Thomas Meinert / pixelio.de

More available books at **www.hansebooks.com**

EGYPTIAN MONUMENTS

This series of 190 Photographs of the various races conquered or visited by the Egyptians, has been taken by Mr. Flinders Petrie from the monuments in 1887, with the assistance of a grant from the British Association. It is now available for students at the cost price of printing copies. Applications should be made for prints to Mr. R. V. Harman, 75 High Street, Bromley, Kent. If a selection is wanted, a set will be sent, any of which can be detached from the titled sheets by the purchaser, at 2s. 3d. per dozen ; those not required should be at once returned in the sheets to Mr. Harman, with the remittance for those kept. If a whole set is wanted, it will be sent pasted on sheets of parchment paper, with printed titles, on receipt of 45s., postage included. With each whole set, a copy of Mr. Petrie's report and Mr. Tomkins' paper on the geographical identifications, will be sent if requested, so far as the number of copies allowed by the British Association will permit.

The Photographs are mainly from plaster casts, and are therefore far clearer than if directly from the stone. Each has the ancient name from the hieroglyphs, and the modern equivalent, so far as the names can be identified. The situation of each sculpture is stated in the report. All are of the XIXth dynasty, and at Thebes, unless stated otherwise in the titles. Where an interrogation is put, either the ancient name is not expressly stated, but is inferred from similar sculptors, or else the modern name is not a certain identification. Where there are various theories on the identifications, the least unlikely has been adopted without any wish to assert its probable truth. The order of arrangement is such as to bring together the various peoples who have resemblances worthy of notice. such as the Punites and Philistines, (Poeni) ; the Tahennu, Hanebu, and Thuirsha ; the Derdeni and Amorites, &c., subject of course to placing those of one name together.

I

263 Khufu khaf
264-5 his servants

Egyptian royal family
Gizeh iv dyn

266-8 His servants Egyptian

Gizeh iv dyn

244-5

244-5 High Egyptian

103

10 Punt Hathor
104 Punt Hathor
5 Cave of Punt

6-8 Chiefs of Pun   Xviii dyn

11S 2   eshfu   la   ay

105 Pun. Memthu   Metae

102 Pun. Chatitum   Settite

II

115 Pun. U... ..

114 Pan Mentu   Mund

113 Pan Utn   Udam

112A Pun. (Name destroyed)

111 Pun. Aar Ara

107 Pun. Ahuul   Avalitis (gr)

106 Pun. Anhimeru   Emmamre

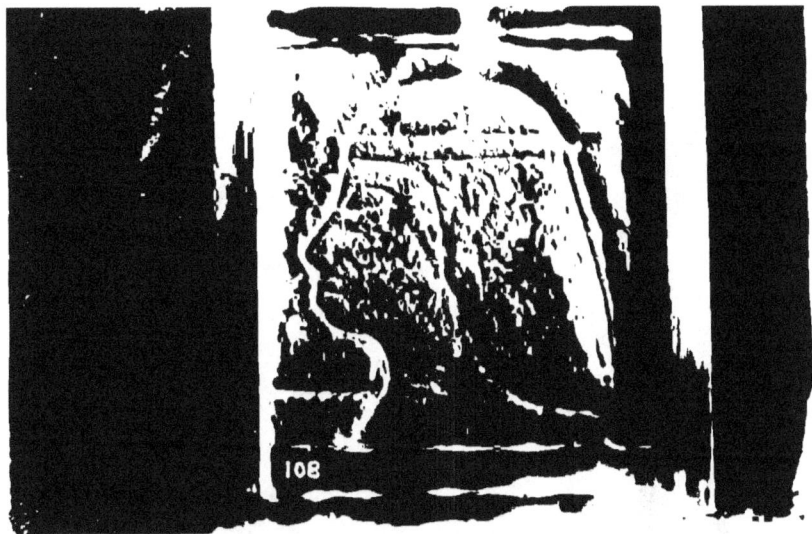

108 Pun. Abes   Abso

109 Pun   Habnu   Heban

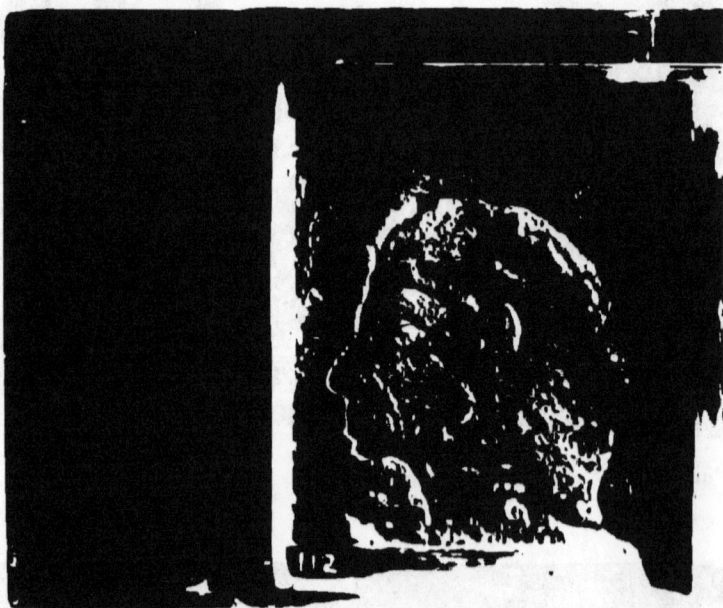

112 Pun. Thenas

III

99 l'un   Antebeth

1-1-2 Pulistha   Philistines xx dyn.

2042-3 Pulistha   Philistine xx dyn

2043-4 Pulistha   Philistines xx dyn

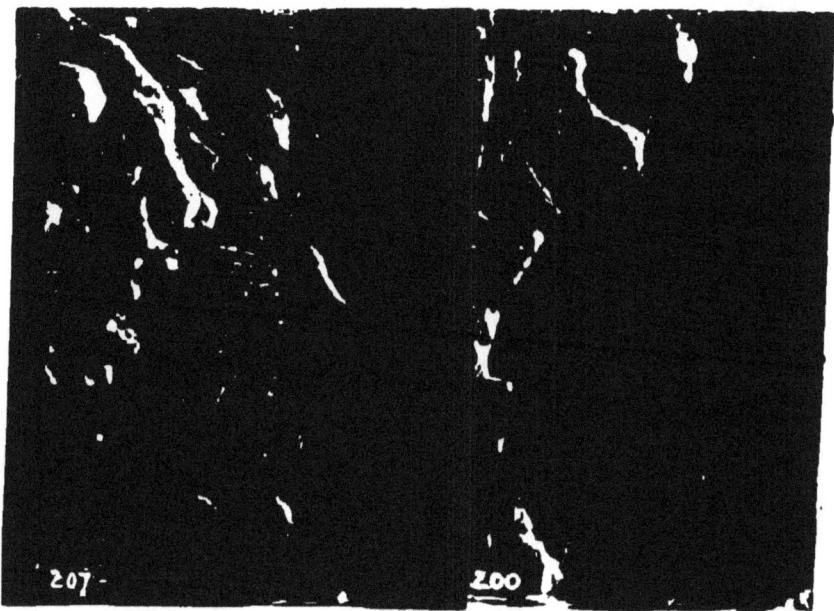

207-200 Shairdana   Sardinian? xx dyn

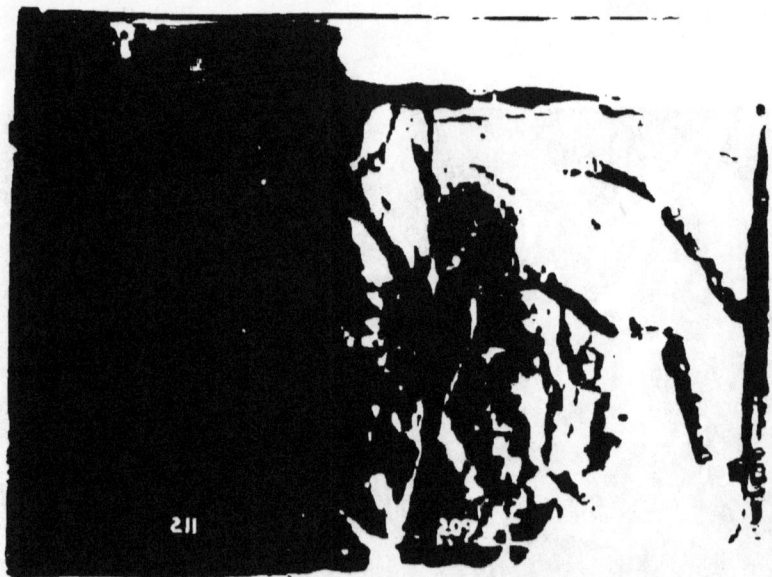

209-211 Shaindaua :

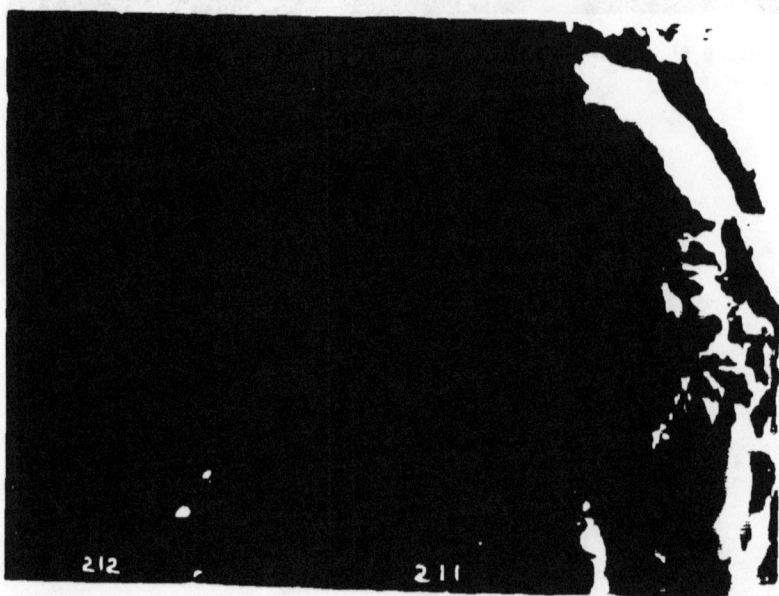

211-2 Sha...

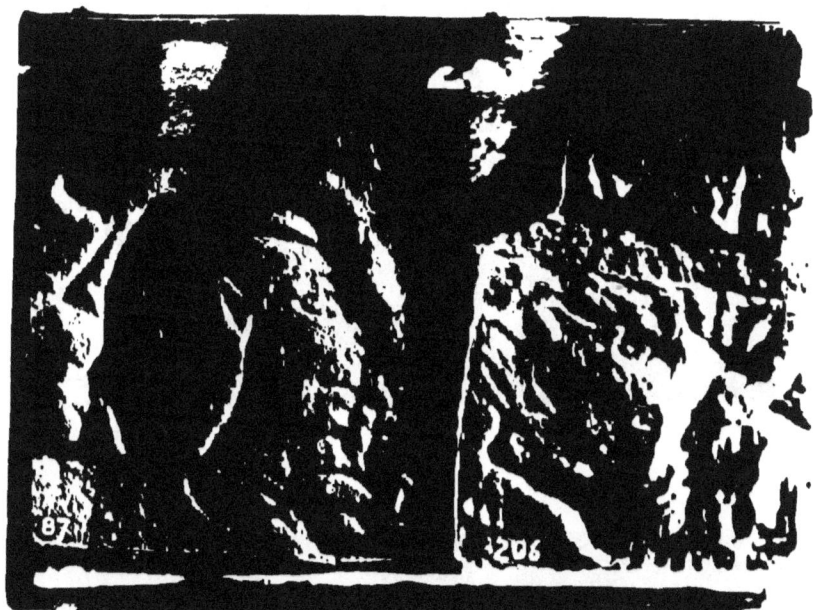

Arm
206 Shairdana ?

Ormah
xx dyn.

210 Shairdana ?

xx dyn.

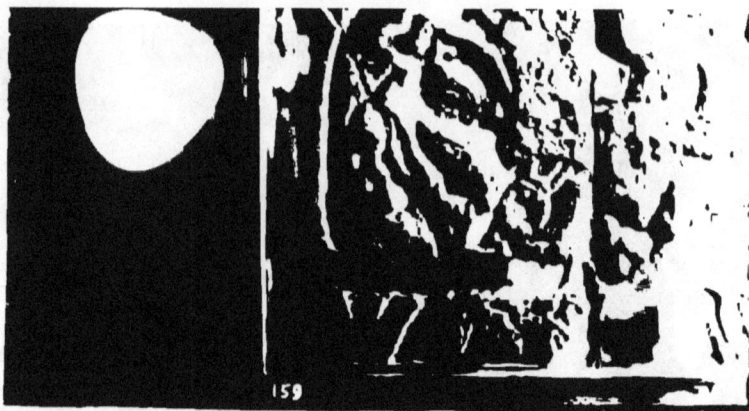

158, 159 Shairdana

Sardinian XX de

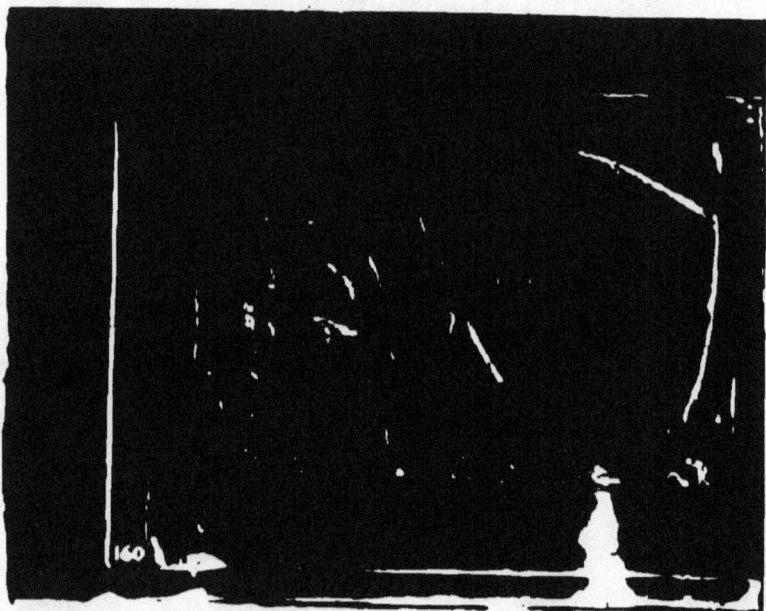

160 Shakals?

lian XX de

IV

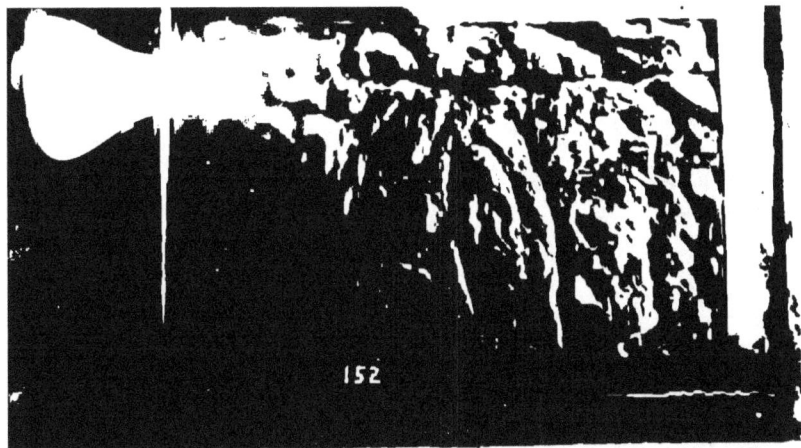

152 Lebu   Libyan xx dyn.

85 Tahennu   Near the Syrtes

96

Tahennu   apparently   neous   x dy

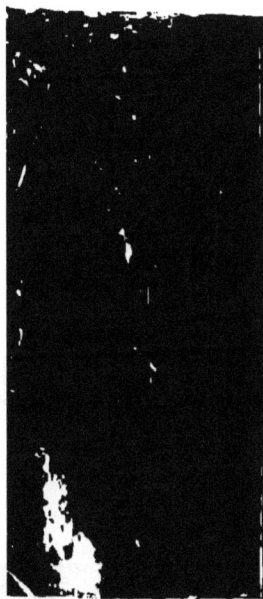

Greek of Europe or Asia

Fo.' Flourish...   Furaos...   Prussians

. ta Mi..   ...paign...   ...remheb, with the Haneba...

V

Asia Minor, in campaign of Horemheb, with the Hittites

2. As above

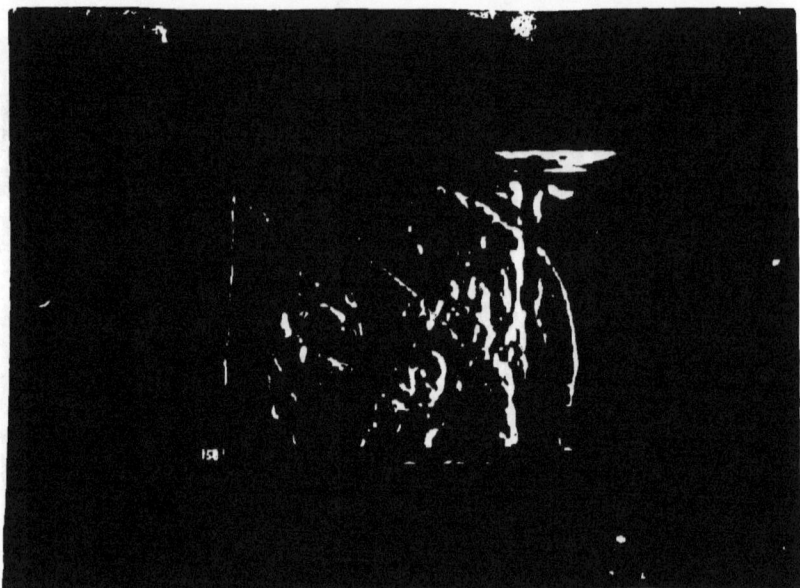

158 Takrur   T... . ... XXdya

168 Takrur
167, 168 Syriane   . dy:

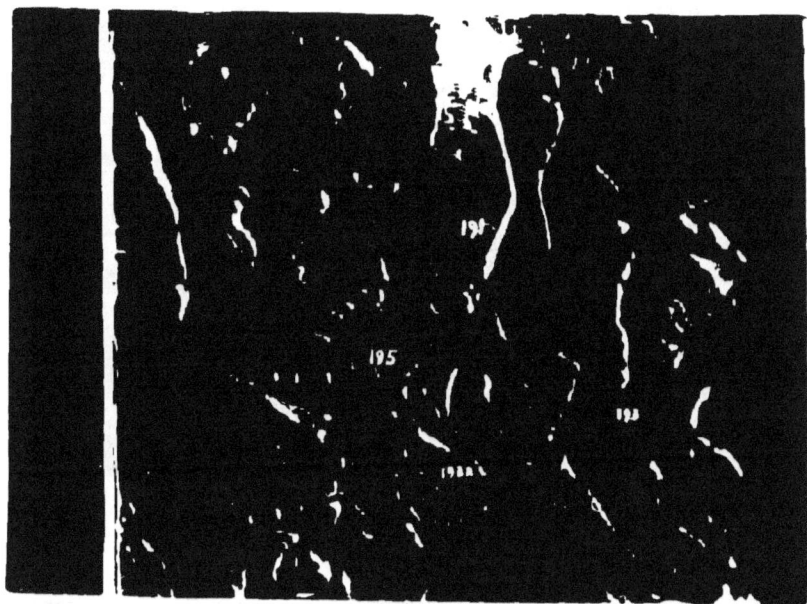

194 Takrui
195 Philistine?

Teukrien
xx dyn

174-7 Takrui

Teukrien xx dyn.

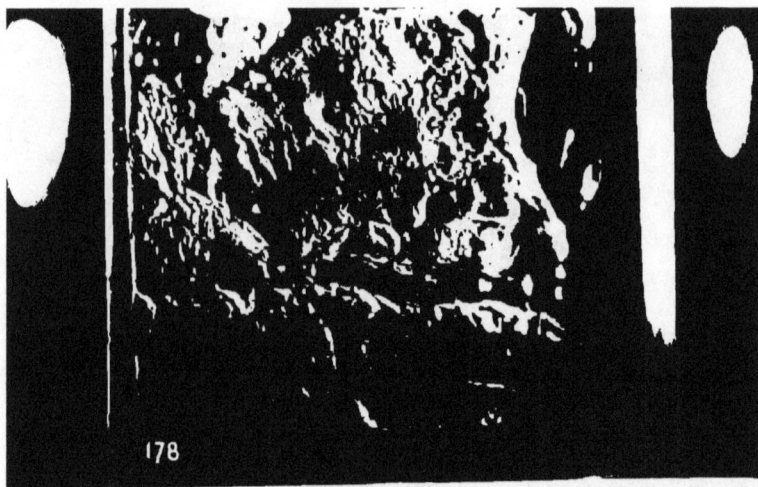

178

11-12

146-8 Amar   Amorites

124 Amur of Dapur   Amorite of Tabor

149 Amar   Amarna

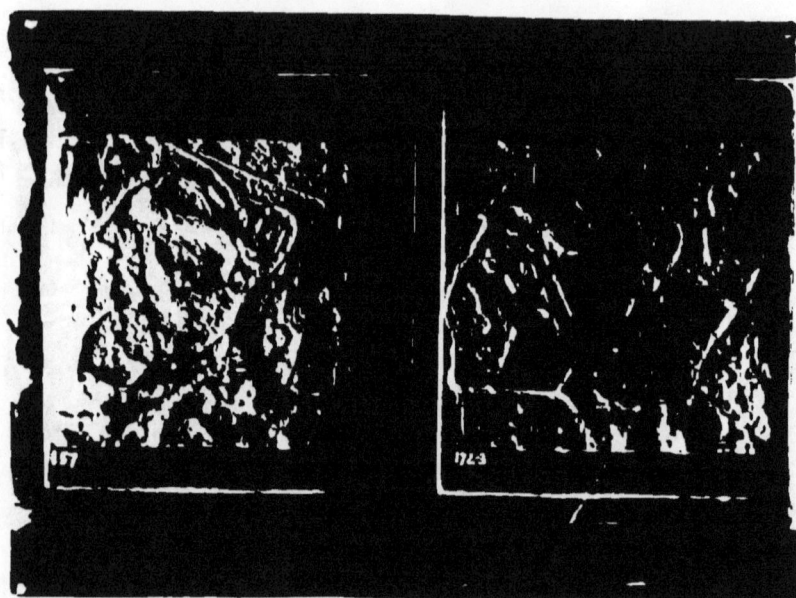

157 Amar
172-3 Syrians   Am. xx dyn.

VI

62 Amar   Amorite

63 Amar   Amorite

Amorito xx dyn

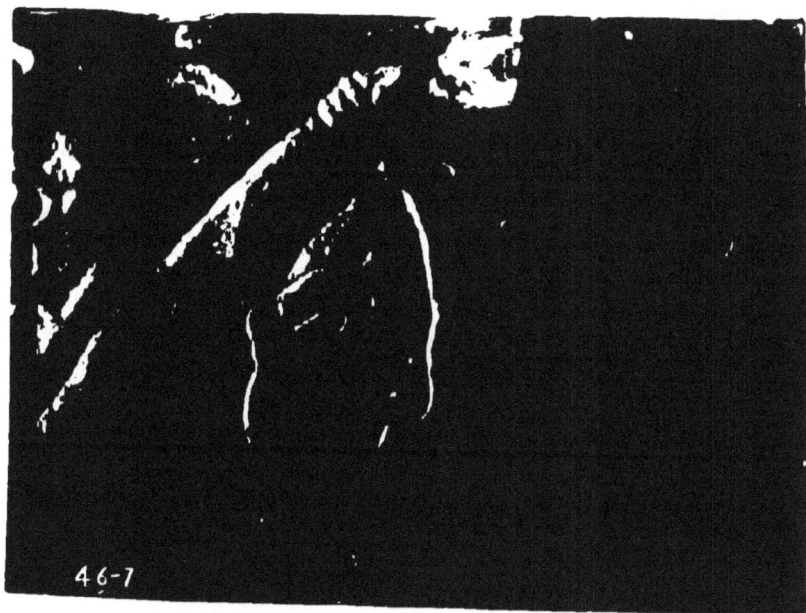

46-7 Shasu   Arabs

46 Shasu   Arabs

"i Shasu t Kanana   Arab of Horbet Knai

42   43

42 3 Shi   Ara's

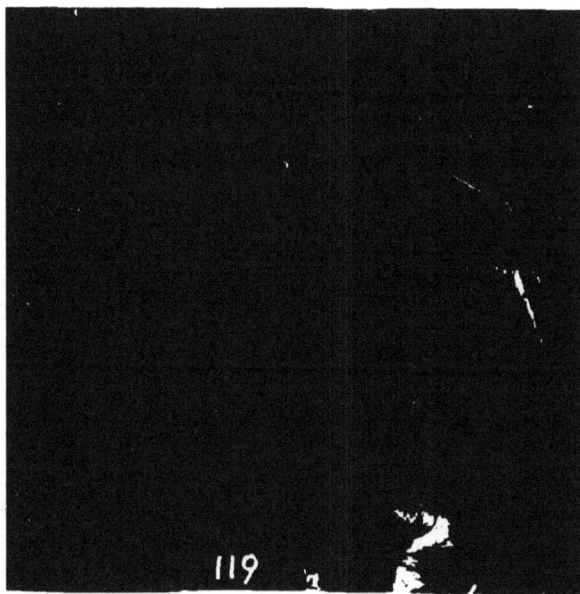

119 Syrian   Typical

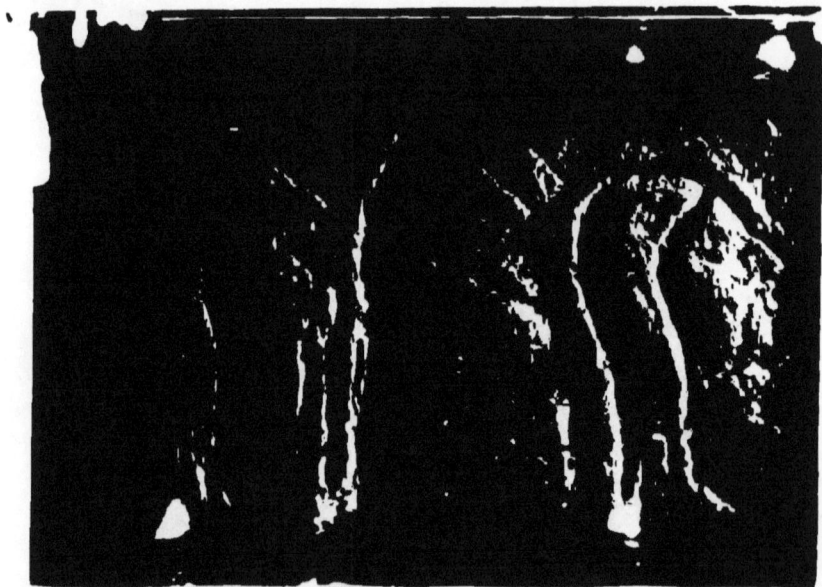

VII

117 Thuesku   Damascu

120 Typical Syrian from Pylon

1 N Syrian   Near **Euphrates**

170-3 Syrian   xx dyn

37 Ganata

Wady ganata xxii dyn.

36 Hanini u

Beit Hanina xxii dyn.

38 Judehmalk   Royal Town in Judea xxii dyn.

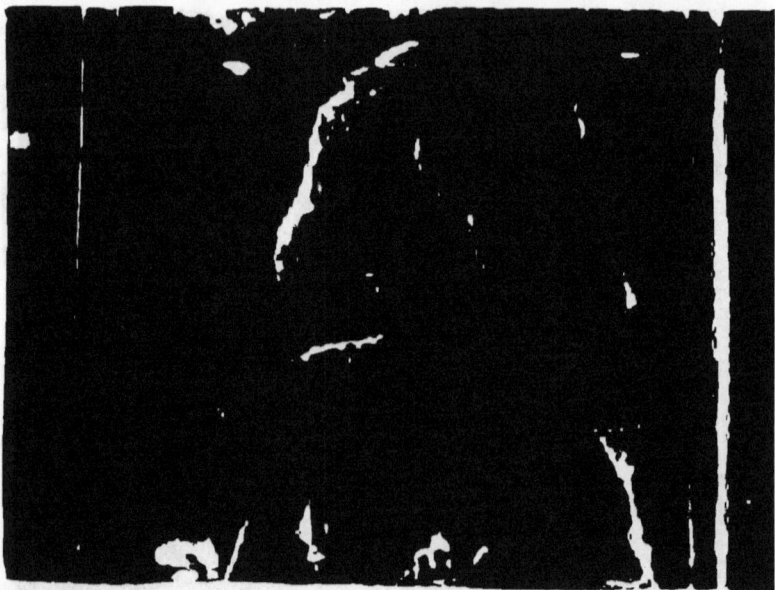

39 Adir   Judah xxii dyn.

24, 29 Near Ataka (N. Syria)

25, 26 Near Leza Kalb Luzeh

241-2 N Syrians

N Syrian

VIII

121 Marma

Merom

122 Marma

Merom

123

123 Martha   Mercula

125, 126 Kur

129 Raur

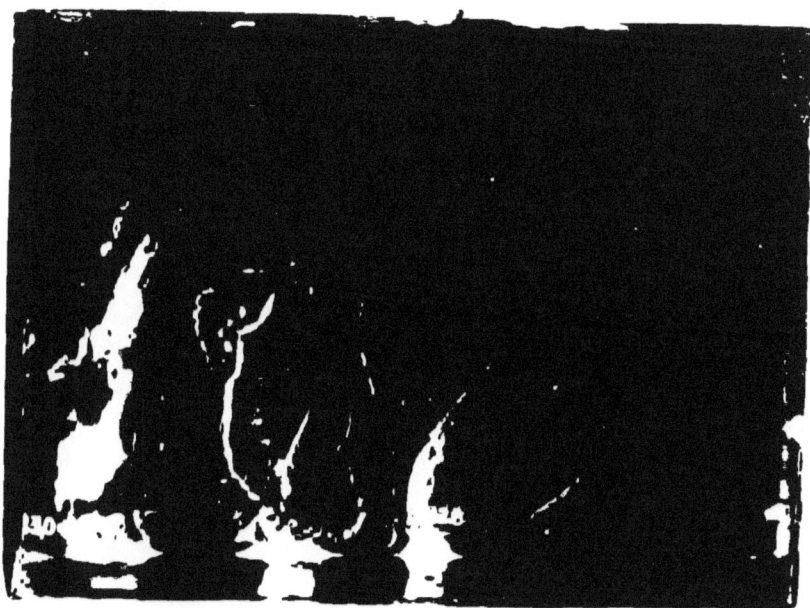

128, 130 Anmaime

132 Kup

Kernen   Kinnzunge

136-7

IX

140 M...pet'a

141 I..p'

22-3 Ai   Kafr Aya

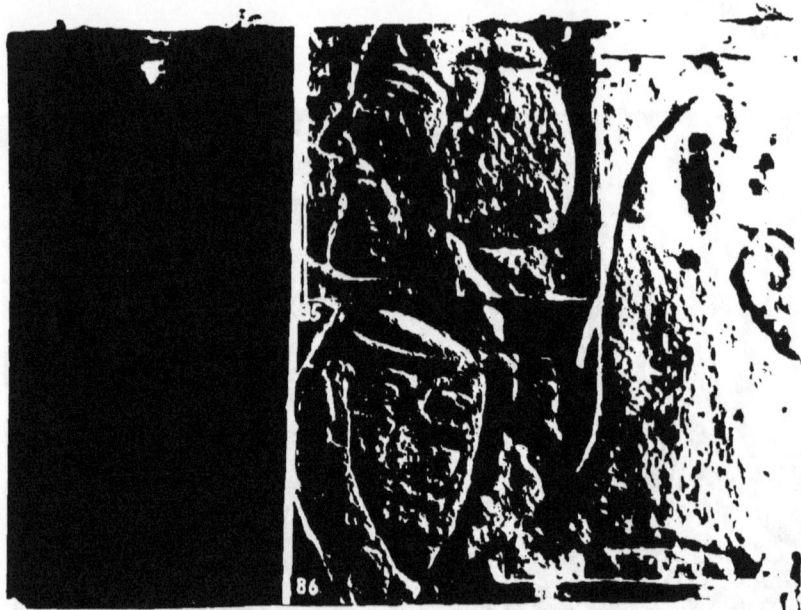

35 S Syrian   Amorite
86 Aleppo

238, 239

X

34

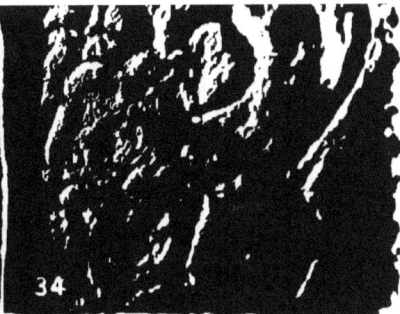

185 N

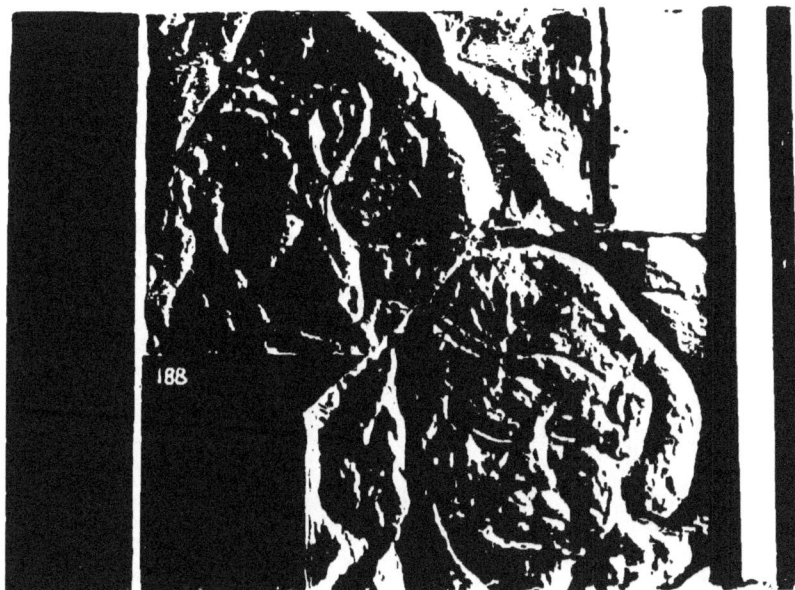

188

187-8 N Syrian

16-17

16, 17 N Syrian
120 Arvioima
88-9 Remenu

Lebanon

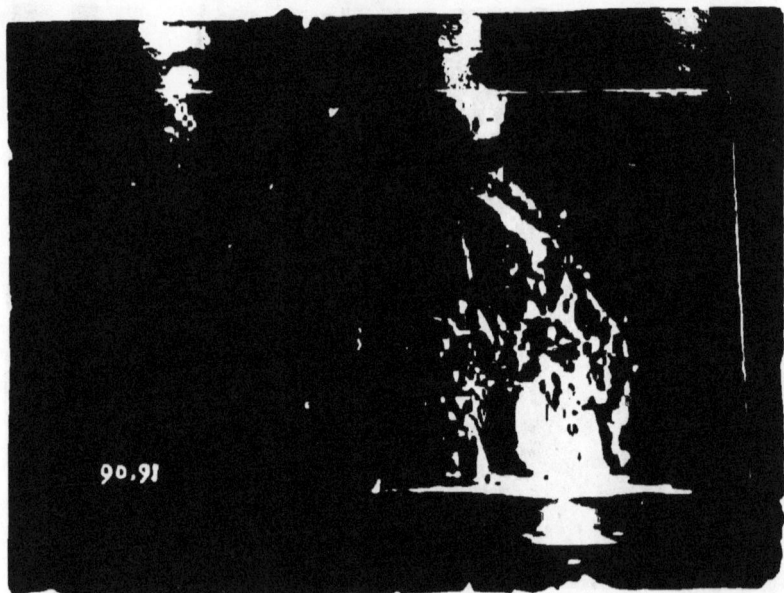

90, 91 Remonen   Lebanon

92, 93 Araban

38 Syrinx

81A Innuas   Enys ?

78, 81c Innuaa   Enya?

79, 81в Innua?   Enya?

XI

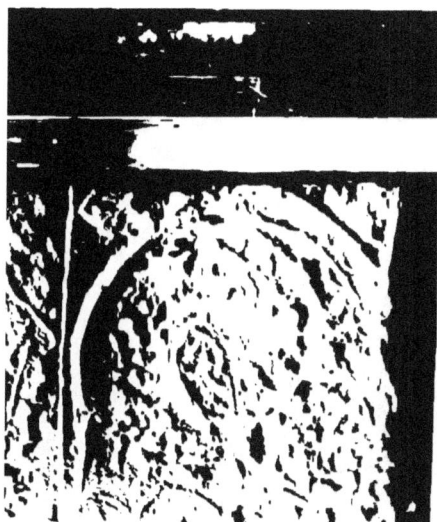

74

73 Rutennu   N. Syria

69 Rutennu   N. Syria

N. Syria

Hittites

49-5

9-51 Khita   Hittites

Hittites

Hittite

XII

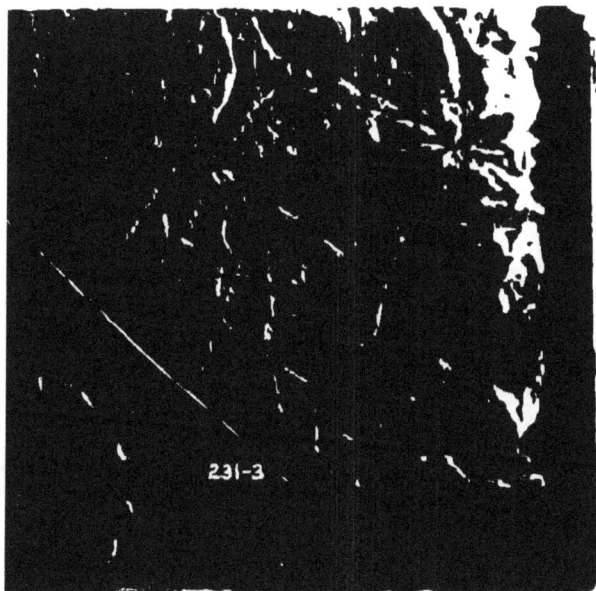

231-3

52-4

Hittites

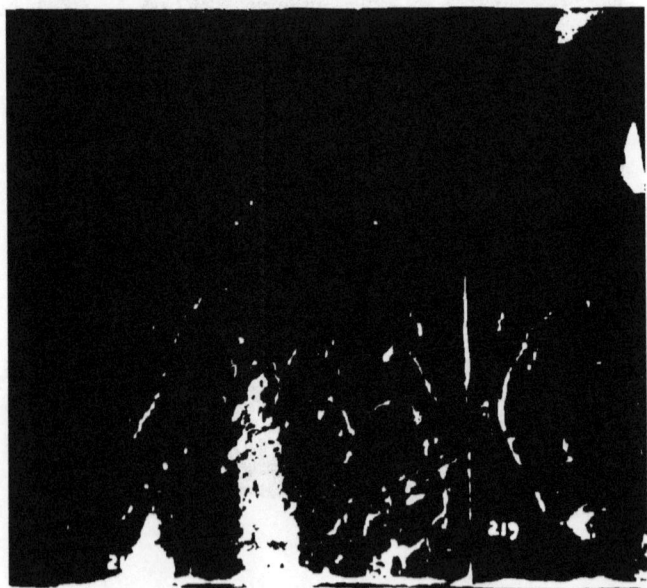

215-8, 219 Hittit - ?

217-8, 262 Hittites

246-253 Hittites?

254-261 Hittites?

228-9 N Sy ians

Br nch of Hittites?

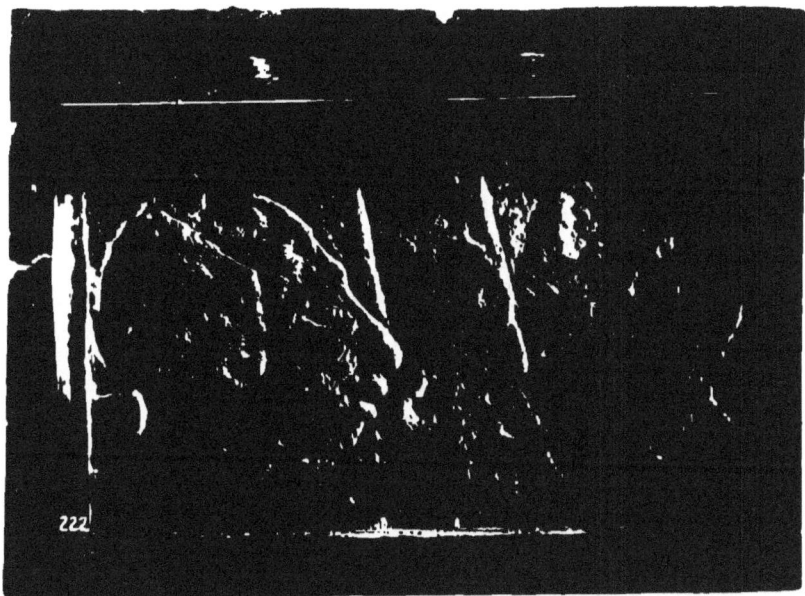

222 N. Syrian   Branch of Hittites ?

150 Kesh   Kush

XIII

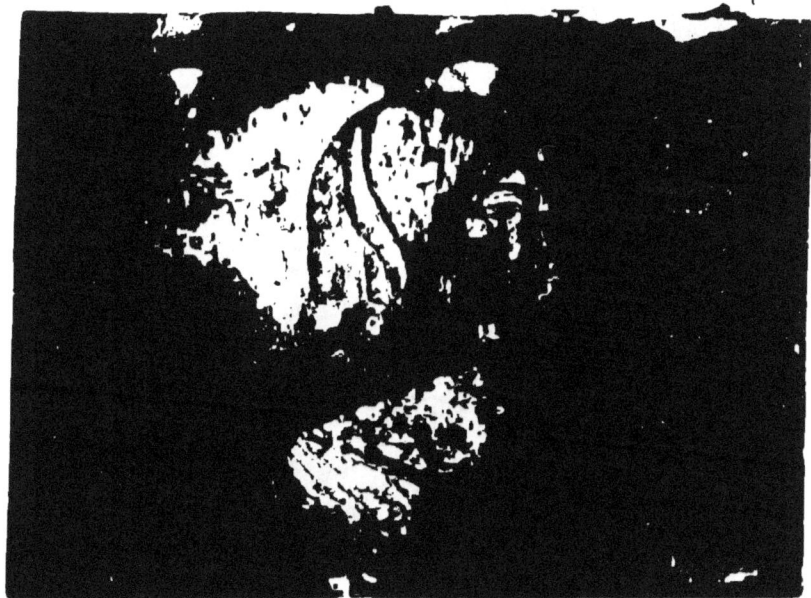

772 **Tomb** of Merenptah   Western race

773 **Tomb** of Merenptah   Southern race

774 Tomb of Merenptah   Northern race

775 Tomb of Merenptah

777 Tomb of Ramessu III. Northern race

778 Tomb of Ramessu III. Southern race

779 Tomb of Ramessu III   Western race

780 Tomb of Ramessu III.   Southern race

776 Tomb of Seti I.   Southern race

781 Tomb of Rekhmara   Brickmakers

610 Khuenaten   Tomb at Yell el Amarna

782 Tomb of Rekhmana   Brickmakers

XIV

794

794 Hyksos Sphinx (See 187 Syrian)   Tanis

795 As above. (See 188 Syrian)

107 Hyksus Chief

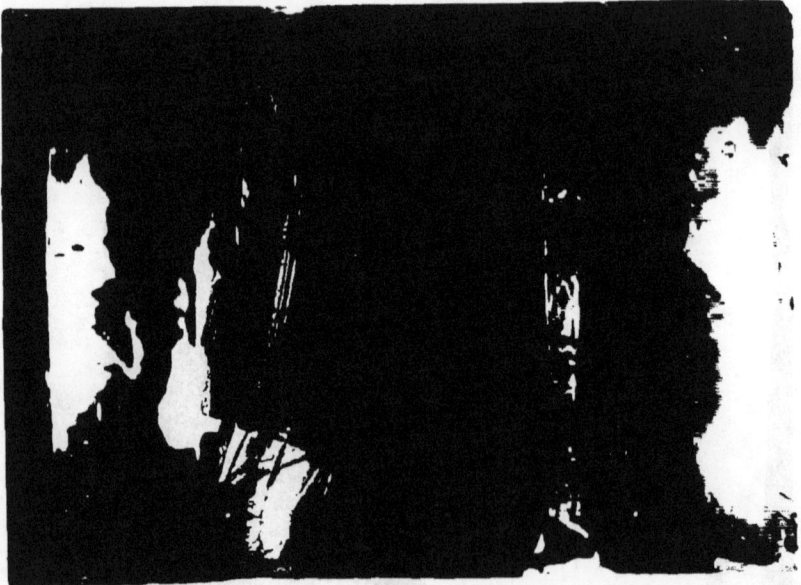

799 Hyksos   Tanis

672 Bearded Servants of Paheri   El Kab

673 Setau and Wife   El Kab

669 Bearded Servants of Pahori

612 People of Khal (Syria) and Kush (Ethiopia)   Tell el Amarna

743 Chiefs of Pun

198, 199 Egyptian Allies

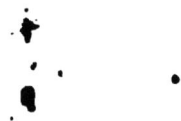

XV

767 Captives led by Ramessu III.   Madinet Habu Top line

768 Captives led by Ramessu III.   Lower line

65 Captives of Ramessu III.   Top and Mid line

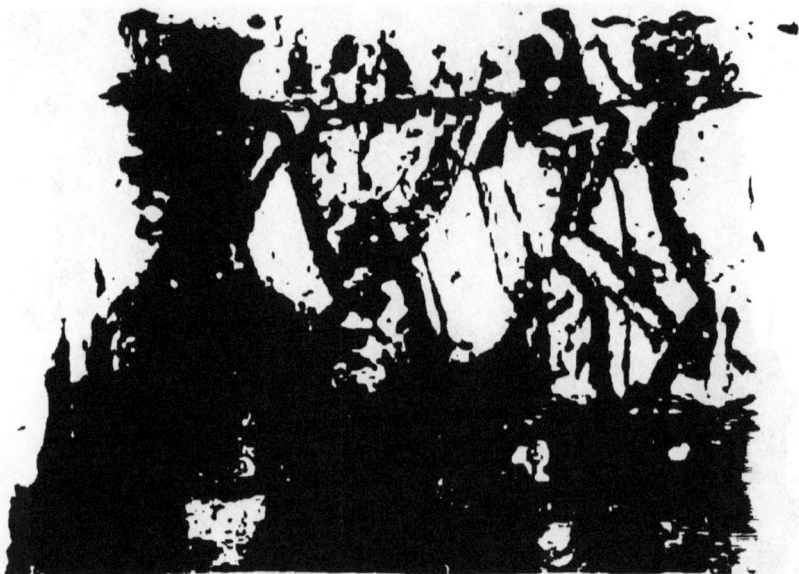

764 Captives of Ramessu III   Mid line

766 Captives of Ramessu III.   Base line

763 Lebu   Libyans

771 Lebu   Slain by Ramessu III.

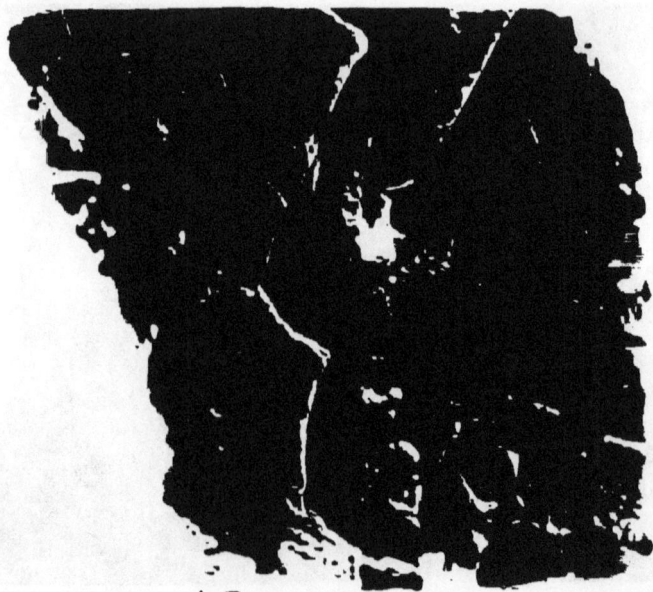

770 As above

753 Siege of Dapur   Ramesseum

755 Drowned Chief of Kita   Ramesseum

748 People of Askalna   Ascalon

XVI

789 Commander of Kush   Chief of Soleb

790 Negroes on Shipboard

792

791

787 People of Auau   Base of above joins 785

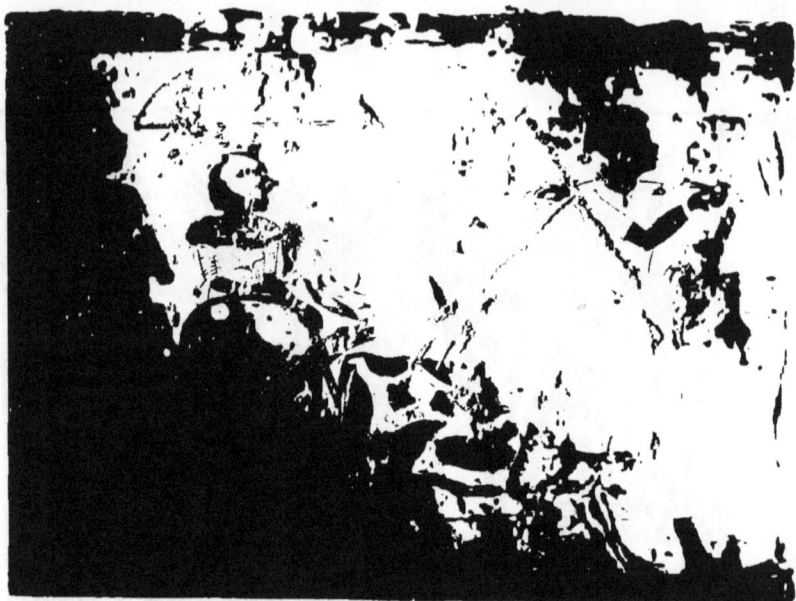

788 Joins 787. Queen in Chariot   Joins 786

785 Joins 787 base   Joins 784

786 Joins 788. Chiefs of Mam and Uaata

784 Joins 785. Chiefs of Kush

78 Golden Cabinet with figures on top

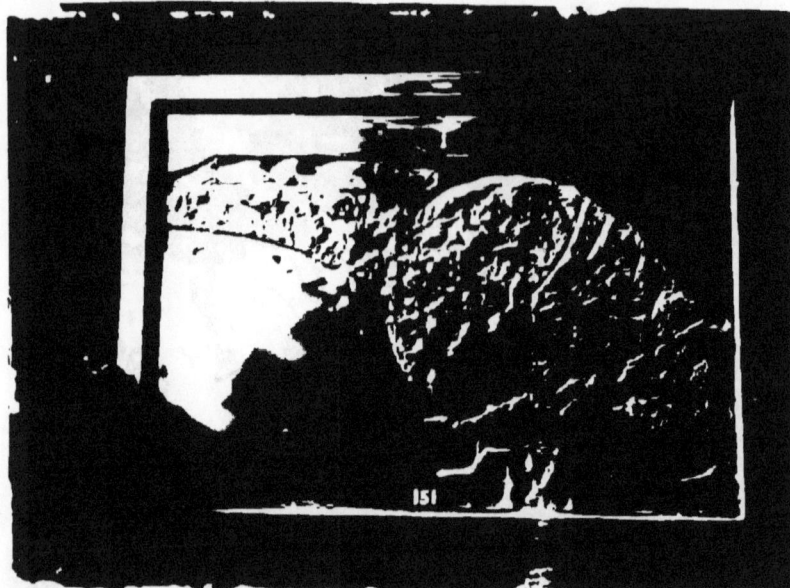

151 Southern Chief (name destroyed)   Medinet Habu

9 783337 240332